GODS, HEROES,
AND MYTHOLOGY

EGYPTIAN
GODS, HEROES,
AND MYTHOLOGY

BY TAMMY GAGNE

CONTENT CONSULTANT
James P. Allen
Wilbour Professor of Egyptology
Brown University

Core Library

An Imprint of Abdo Publishing
abdobooks.com

Cover image: Anubis is one of the most widely
recognized Egyptian gods.

abdocorelibrary.com

Published by Abdo Publishing, a division of ABDO, PO Box 398166,
Minneapolis, Minnesota 55439. Copyright © 2019 by Abdo Consulting
Group, Inc. International copyrights reserved in all countries. No part of this
book may be reproduced in any form without written permission from the
publisher. Core Library™ is a trademark and logo of Abdo Publishing.

Printed in the United States of America, North Mankato, Minnesota
092018
012019

THIS BOOK CONTAINS
RECYCLED MATERIALS

Cover Photo: Paolo Gallo/Shutterstock Images
Interior Photos: Paolo Gallo/Shutterstock Images, 1; Dean Mouhtaropoulos/Getty Images
News/Getty Images, 4–5, 43; Shutterstock Images, 7 (foreground), 24–25, 26, 35, 36–37, 45;
iStockphoto, 7 (background); DeAgostini/Getty Images, 8, 21, 30–31, 33; Nano Calvo/VWPics/
AP Images, 11 (top right); Natalya Okorokova/Shutterstock Images, 11 (middle right), 11 (bottom
right); Marco Sardi/Shutterstock Images, 11 (left); Album/Metropolitan Museum of Art, NY/
Newscom, 14–15, 19; Patrick Landmann/Science Source, 17; DEA Picture Library/De Agostini/Getty
Images, 22; Anton Ivanov/Shutterstock Images, 40

Editor: Marie Pearson
Series Designer: Ryan Gale

Library of Congress Control Number: 2018949772

Publisher's Cataloging-in-Publication Data

Names: Gagne, Tammy, author.
Title: Egyptian gods, heroes, and mythology / by Tammy Gagne.
Description: Minneapolis, Minnesota : Abdo Publishing, 2019 | Series: Gods, heroes, and
    mythology | Includes online resources and index.
Identifiers: ISBN 9781532117817 (lib. bdg.) | ISBN 9781532170676 (ebook)
Subjects: LCSH: Egyptian mythology--Juvenile literature. | Gods, Egyptian--Juvenile
    literature. | Heroes--Juvenile literature.
Classification: DDC 299.31--dc23

CONTENTS

HOW OSIRIS CAME TO RULE THE DEAD

The god Osiris was a great ruler of Egypt. Seth, his brother, was jealous. Seth wanted the throne for himself. He made a plan. During a party at the king's palace, Seth suggested that everyone play a game. He placed a large chest in front of all the guests. He invited them to climb into it to see who would fit. He knew that Osiris would fit just right. When the unknowing king got inside, his scheming brother slammed the lid shut.

Osiris is often portrayed with green skin and his legs wrapped like a mummy's.

Osiris was trapped. Without enough air to breathe, the king soon died.

Seth dumped the chest into the Nile River. He hoped that it would sink to the bottom. But instead, it floated all the way to the Mediterranean Sea. The king's wife, Isis, wanted to give her husband a proper burial. Without it, he could not move into the afterlife. She set off in search of the chest.

After much searching, Isis finally found the chest. But Seth was waiting when she returned to Egypt. He watched as she hid

CLEOPATRA AND ISIS

By the year 332 BCE, Greek rulers led Egypt. Cleopatra was a popular Greek queen who ruled Egypt. She often dressed and acted like the goddess Isis. This was no accident. The more the ancient Egyptians related her to the goddess, the more powerful she became as a ruler. Many of her subjects believed the queen was in fact Isis reborn.

Seth was the primary god of Upper Egypt in the south.

the chest in the marshes along the river. And as soon as she left, he retrieved it. Seth was determined to keep Isis from burying her husband. Trying to sink the chest had not worked. So he decided to separate the king's body into pieces. He thought scattering the remains would ensure that the queen could never find every piece. But she did not give up. She hunted down all the pieces. She gave each one a sacred burial of its own. This allowed Osiris's soul to move into the afterlife. There, he became the king of the dead.

Then, Isis gave birth to Horus, Osiris's son. Horus was the rightful heir to the throne. This fact would likely make him Seth's next victim. Isis hid Horus from Seth until Horus grew up. Then, Horus was able to take his father's place on the throne.

EGYPTIAN MYTHOLOGY

This myth of Osiris is one of many stories in Egyptian mythology. Stories like this one tell us how the ancient

Egyptians depicted Isis, *left*, and Osiris, *center*, on their coffins.

Egyptians understood the world. The ancient Egyptians were polytheistic. That means they believed in many gods. They had more than 2,000 different gods and goddesses. Each helped explain something about the world. Followers focused on the deities that could affect their lives the most. A person who fished for food in the Nile likely prayed to Sebek, the crocodile god.

There are many different versions of Egyptian myths. This is because the myths were told by word of mouth long before they were ever written down. People in different regions of Egypt told and retold the stories for more than 3,000 years. Details sometimes changed. Eventually, people began recording them in writing.

The ancient Egyptian writing system used symbols called hieroglyphs. Hieroglyphs were carved into artifacts, including objects made of wood and stone. One famous artifact is the Rosetta stone. Over time, archaeologists found several ancient texts that tell the stories of Egyptian mythology. They include the Pyramid

ROSETTA STONE
TEXT

The Rosetta stone included three different scripts that were used in Egypt when the carving was made. Hieroglyphs were on the top. A cursive form of hieroglyphs called demotic was in the middle. Greek script was at the bottom. Why do you think the text needed to be written in three different scripts?

Hieroglyphs

Demotic

Greek

THE ROSETTA STONE

Ancient Egyptian hieroglyphs were picture-like symbols that stood for people, places, and ideas. For a long time, archaeologists could not read Egyptian hieroglyphs. In 1799, a French soldier was working near the town of Rosetta, Egypt. He found a large stone with writing on it. Later it was called the Rosetta stone. The stone had been carved in approximately 196 BCE. It had a message written by Egyptian priests. The same message was written in three different scripts. These were the Greek alphabet, Egyptian hieroglyphs, and a cursive form of Egyptian hieroglyphs called demotic. Archaeologists knew the Greek alphabet. They used the Greek to decode the meaning of the hieroglyphs.

Texts, the Book of the Dead, and a group of general texts called the Underworld Books.

Ancient Egyptian mythology told about an afterlife. When wealthy people died, their families had the bodies mummified, or preserved. Ancient Egyptians believed preserving the body made it possible for a person's soul to live forever.

STRAIGHT TO THE
SOURCE

Geraldine Pinch is the author of *Egyptian Myth: A Very Short Introduction*. In this book, she explains why experts disagree about the definition of a myth.

> *There is disagreement among Egyptologists about when mythical narratives first developed in Egypt. This dispute is partly due to the difficulty of deciding what should be counted as a myth. Today, the term myth is often used in a negative way to refer to something that is exaggerated or untrue. In ancient cultures, myth did not have this negative connotation; myths could be regarded as stories that contained poetic rather than literal truths. Some scholars separate myths from other types of traditional tale by classifying them as stories featuring deities. This simple definition might work quite well for Egypt, but not for all cultures.*

> Source: Geraldine Pinch. *Egyptian Myth: A Very Short Introduction*. New York: Oxford University Press, 2004. Print. 1–2.

What's the Big Idea?

Take a close look at Pinch's words. What is her main idea? What evidence does she use to support her point? Explain in a few sentences how the author uses evidence to support her main point.

EGYPTIAN GODS AND GODDESSES

One of the most widely worshipped Egyptian deities is the sun god Ra. The ancient Egyptians saw Ra as the source of all life. Before him, all that existed was just water, everywhere—a universal ocean. Then a space formed in the water. In that space Ra, a sun god, appeared. He was in the form of a shining bird. After that, Ra was reborn each morning to his mother, the sky goddess.

Ra created the rest of the world. He then ruled this space. Ra also became king of all

Ra, *left,* often had the head of a falcon and a solar disc over his head.

HOLDING ONTO BELIEFS

In the 1300s BCE, a king named Akhenaten ruled Egypt. He tried to convince his subjects to abolish all gods but one. He wanted the people to worship a single god named Aten, a sun god. This idea was not popular with the Egyptian people. They continued to believe in many different gods and goddesses.

other Egyptian gods. Ancient Egyptian rulers were said to be the sons of Ra.

THE MOST REVERED

As the god of the dead, Osiris played a vital role in Egyptian mythology. He was also closely linked with Egypt's pharaohs. Upon death, a king was believed to become Osiris. The new king became the god Horus. Horus was often shown as a falcon. Artists depicted kings with a falcon over their heads. One very important Egyptian goddess was Isis. As a wife and mother, she was a role model for Egyptian women.

Gods and goddesses such as Isis, *right*, were closely associated with Egyptian royalty, including queen Nefertari, *left*.

GODS WITH ANIMAL HEADS

Many Egyptian gods and goddesses have animal heads. The animal features symbolized different traits each god shared with a particular animal. Depicting gods with animal features helped people see them as stronger and scarier. A god with the head of a jackal or a lion commanded more respect and fear than a god who looked like a human being. These forms also made gods easier to identify for people who could not read their names.

Seth was another important Egyptian god. His actions helped explain the violence that existed in the world. Some Egyptians saw violence as a necessary part of life. One Egyptian pharaoh, King Peribsen, identified himself with Seth instead of Horus.

MAAT

The word *maat* means "truth and justice." These were important concepts to ancient Egyptians. All Egyptian rulers were expected to speak the truth and rule fairly. If they did not, they would be judged harshly in the afterlife.

A person's heart, *left side of scale*, was weighed against Maat, *right side of scale*, to determine if that person had upheld truth and justice.

Maat, the daughter of Ra, was the goddess of truth and justice. She brought order to the world. According to Egyptian myths, she also balanced the scales of justice in the afterlife. When people died, their hearts were weighed on these scales. This revealed whether or not that person had lived a righteous life.

ANUBIS

When ancient Egyptians died, their family and friends prayed to Anubis. Anubis was the first god of the dead. Then Osiris came to rule the afterlife. Anubis brought the dead to him for the heart-weighing ceremony.

Anubis had a jackal's head paired with a human's body. Some Egyptian art shows him entirely in animal form. When Egyptian priests attended funerals, they often wore masks of Anubis. They did this to protect the deceased person from real jackals, which often tried to steal bodies from burial sites.

BASTET

Bastet was a cat goddess known mainly in the city of Bubastis. She became an important deity of Egyptian kings. A daughter of Ra, Bastet had many qualities of a mother cat. She was kind to the kings and fierce to their enemies. Like Anubis, Bastet had a human body with an animal's head. Early art showed her with the head of a lion. Later, her head looked more like that of a housecat.

Anubis had long, pointy ears.

Drawings and sculptures of Bastet often included her kittens as well.

Ancient Egyptians valued cats greatly. Some owners buried their dead cats in cemeteries. In the

Bastet can appear as a cat or as a human with a cat head.

1960s, the Egyptian Antiquities Service dug up several cat cemeteries. They found mummified cats. They also found many bronze statues of the cat goddess and her kittens. These sculptures became popular with antique collectors.

STRAIGHT TO THE
SOURCE

Edmund Meltzer is an Egyptologist, a person who studies the culture of ancient Egypt. In an interview, he explained the concept of Maat in Egyptian mythology:

It is also a fundamental aspect of Maat that balance is maintained or restored, and oppositions are reconciled. Thus, in the struggle between Horus and Set[h], after Set[h] murders Osiris, the final decision awarding the kingship to Horus is enacted by a legal decision of the gods, not the result of a fight to the death (though Horus and Set[h] fought for a long time and inflicted grievous injuries on one another). The two gods are reconciled, albeit tensely. Law and justice pervade the other world as well as this world—when Maat is in her proper place, that is.

Source: Nikole Hollenitsch. "Mythology, Cosmology, and Symbolism of Ancient Egypt, Part 1." *Pacifica Post*. Pacifica Graduate Institute, January 30, 2018. Web. Accessed July 3, 2018.

Back It Up
The authors of this passage are using evidence to support a point. Write a paragraph describing the point the authors are making. Then write down two or three pieces of evidence the authors use to make the point.

CREATURES OF EGYPTIAN MYTHOLOGY

One of the most famous creatures in Egyptian mythology is the sphinx. Sphinxes are common in Egyptian art. A sphinx has the body of a lion. Its head may be that of a ram, a hawk, or a human being. Many sphinx sculptures had the heads of Egyptian kings or queens. This depiction helped the rulers seem more powerful to the people.

When many people think of sphinxes, they picture the Great Sphinx. People travel from all over the world to see this giant sculpture in Giza, Egypt. It is 66 feet (20 m) high

A king's crown had a cobra on the front.

GREAT SPHINX SIZE

66 feet (20 meters)

240 feet (73 meters)

The Great Sphinx of Giza is 240 feet (73 m) long and 66 feet (20 m) high. How do you think people felt when they saw this massive sculpture in ancient times? How might it have made them feel about Egyptian rulers?

and 240 feet (73 m) long. Egyptians carved this sphinx out of a single piece of limestone sometime between 2575 and 2465 BCE, during the reign of King Khafre. Archaeologists believe it depicts either Khafre or his father, Khufu. The Great Sphinx was once colorfully painted. Time has eroded the paint and outer layers of the magnificent statue. It lost its nose hundreds of years ago.

GRIFFINS

Another Egyptian creature is the griffin. It has the body of a lion and the head of a bird, usually an eagle. Sometimes it also has the wings of an eagle. Ancient Egyptians combined the features of these animals for a reason. Both animals are capable hunters. Combining the two made the griffin an ideal symbol of war.

Griffins are often seen in Egyptian art alongside sphinxes. Both are sometimes found at the entrances

WHAT IS THAT?

The god Seth is depicted with animal features. Archaeologists do not know exactly what animal he is supposed to be. Pictures show Seth with a long, curved snout. His ears are long and stand up straight and are flat on top. Sometimes he is also shown with a body like a dog's and a forked tail. Some people think he resembles an okapi, a mammal related to a giraffe. Others say the odd features may not be from any one animal. People may have drawn Seth with parts of different animals mixed together to make him look as disturbing as possible.

to important tombs. There, they serve as guards for the dead.

URAEUS

Snakes were common in ancient Egypt. People living at this time likely saw snakes in the fields where they grew crops. Venomous snakes, such as the cobra, could kill an adult human. For this reason, the snake was both feared and respected.

In Egyptian myths, the cobra was linked to the goddess Wadjet. Her job was to protect the king. The image of an upright cobra was worn on the crowns of Egyptian rulers. This cobra symbol

THE ROLES OF BIG CATS

Big cats were important symbols in Egyptian mythology. Lions, for example, stood for the power of the king or queen. This is why sphinxes were shown with the lion's body. Male leopards were often linked to Seth's rage. Female leopards, on the other hand, were commonly seen as protectors and guardians.

was called a uraeus. It was believed to spit venom at enemies who approached the king.

A SACRED BIRD

The bird called the Benu appears in some Egyptian stories. It is a form of the god Ra. Egyptians taught that the Benu landed on the very first piece of solid ground. This act represented the first time sunlight hit the land.

EXPLORE ONLINE

Chapter Three discusses creatures in Egyptian mythology. The website below goes into detail about the importance of cats for ancient Egyptians. How is the information from the website similar to the information in this book? What new information did you learn from the website?

CATS RULE IN ANCIENT EGYPT
abdocorelibrary.com/egyptian-mythology

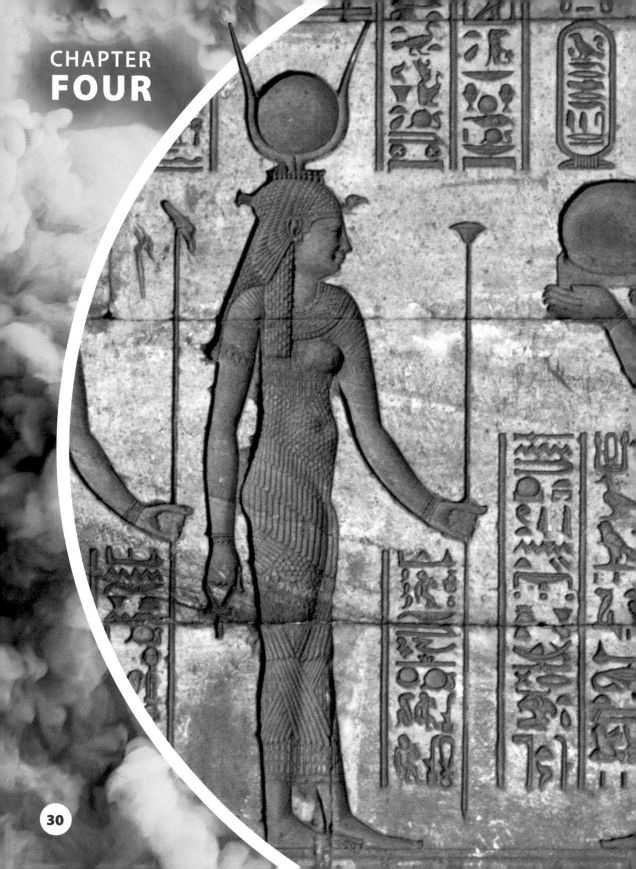

NOTABLE STORIES

According to Egyptian mythology, the Eye of Ra was separate from the sun god Ra. This body part acted entirely on its own. Some stories say the Eye of Ra was his daughter. She protected Ra. In some myths, this goddess is depicted as Hathor, the Egyptian goddess of love. Other stories call her Bastet or Wadjet. Still others identify her as Mut, the mother goddess.

The Eye of Ra can be loving or hateful. The ancient Egyptians believed that all the gods and other living things formed in the pupil of

Hathor, *left*, was associated with the cow. She sometimes had the horns of a cow on her head.

the Eye of Ra. But some stories state that human beings were created from her tears.

THE SOUL'S JOURNEY TO THE AFTERLIFE

The ancient Egyptians believed every person's soul was made up of multiple parts. Two important parts were the *ba* and the *ka*. The ba was the being of a person without the body. After a person died, the ba could leave the tomb and fly away. The ba was often shown as a bird with a human head. The ka was the force of life inside the body. It made the difference between a living person and a dead one.

MAGICIAN HEROES

Heroes from many cultures are usually skilled warriors. But Egyptian heroes are known for using magic instead. In one myth, a priest learned that his wife was in love with another man. He made a wax crocodile and brought it to life to attack the man. Another hero used magic on an injured goose. The bird's head had been separated from its body. This man was able to reattach the bird's head to its body to save its life.

The ba was often shown above a preserved body.

The Egyptians believed that the ka survived after a person's death. For example, it could reside in pictures or statues of that person.

Surviving family members filled tombs with many earthly objects. Objects could include clothes, jewelry, and furniture. The dead would need these objects in the afterlife. Ancient Egyptians believed people with these items would enjoy an afterlife with fewer hardships.

The tombs of kings also housed everything the king would need in the afterlife. Many tombs held valuable items made from gold. Some kings' tombs were inside pyramids. These massive structures were built to honor kings and queens. People believed that kings were gods. After death, they would still have power on earth. They could help the living people they had left behind.

> ## DEITY HEROES
> The ancient Egyptians believed that the gods were superior to humans. Egyptian myths rarely feature human heroes. Instead, these stories almost always focus on the powers of the gods and goddesses. This focus shifts the listener's attention to the power of the deities.

THE SHIPWRECKED SAILOR

The story of the shipwrecked sailor shows the importance of being thankful to the gods. In the story, an Egyptian man's boat sinks in the Red Sea. He finds himself on a deserted island. When he finds food, he thanks the gods for providing for him. He did not

The Red Sea lies between several countries. Egypt, Sudan, and Eritrea are to the west, and Saudi Arabia and Yemen are to the east.

expect to find anything to eat. He also does not expect a god to appear before him. But one does. It is a giant snake with a human head. The god tells the man that he will return home to his loved ones. The god assures him that he will never spend another day in this place. Soon, a ship sails by and rescues the man.

In this myth, the snake is a form of Ra. The human hero of the story doesn't do anything spectacular. He does not fight any monsters or show great strength. He doesn't even have a name. He simply shows gratitude for what the gods have given him. The story also teaches the value of perseverance: never losing hope or determination, no matter how bad things might seem.

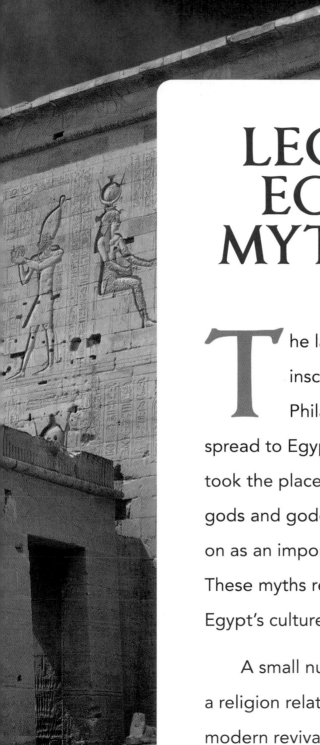

LEGACY OF EGYPTIAN MYTHOLOGY

The last known hieroglyphs were inscribed in 394 CE at the Temple of Philae. By that time, Christianity had spread to Egypt. Christianity, and later Islam, took the place of worshipping the Egyptian gods and goddesses. Still, the mythology lived on as an important part of Egyptian history. These myths remain an important part of Egypt's culture.

A small number of followers still practice a religion related to Egyptian mythology. This modern revival is called Kemetism. The word

The Temple of Philae is on an island in the Nile River.

Kemet was an old word that meant "Egypt." Although the religion is not widely practiced, it has added to modern fascination with Egyptian culture around the world. The singer Rihanna has tattoos of an Egyptian falcon and the goddess Isis. Rap artist Kanye West sometimes wears a pendant with the image of Horus.

SCARAB BEETLES

Insects called scarab beetles were important to ancient Egyptians. They believed that these beetles were linked to Khepri, the god of the early morning sun. They wrote his name with the scarab hieroglyph. Carvings of these beetles date back to 2575 BCE. Scarabs are still popular in art and jewelry today.

TOURISM

The last Egyptian temple closed for worship in the 500s CE. But many temples and other ancient structures have become huge tourist attractions in the modern era. The pyramids and the Great Sphinx of Giza are among the most popular sites. The Great Temples of Hatshepsut, a queen who reigned from 1473 to 1458 BCE, are grand structures.

So is the Temple of Amenhotep III, king from 1390 to 1353 BCE. Both sites attract much attention from historians and travelers. Temples like these were built so people could honor the kings after their deaths.

Modern Egyptians still value ancient structures. The Abu Simbel temple is a great example. Built to honor King Ramses II, this temple was at risk of being destroyed in the 1960s. The construction of the Aswan Dam on the Nile meant that the structure would soon be underwater. To prevent its demise, the United Nations Educational, Scientific and Cultural Organization (UNESCO) got involved.

ANCIENT CELEBRATIONS

The ancient Egyptian calendar included many festivals. Scrolls have been found that list the dates and descriptions of various festivals. The walls of certain temples offer more information about these celebrations. Few are still celebrated today. But thanks to the hieroglyphs on these walls, we now have a much greater understanding of them.

Workers moved the entire temple to a location out of the water's reach. The project took four years to finish.

The myths that once ruled life for ancient Egyptians are no longer at the center of everyday life in this region. But their influence on architecture, art, and history is undeniable. These stories remain a treasured resource for the nation of Egypt and the rest of the world.

FURTHER EVIDENCE

Chapter Five discusses various facts about ancient Egyptian culture. What is the main idea of this chapter? What key evidence supports this idea? Take a look at the website below. Find information from the site that supports the main idea of this chapter. Does the information support an existing piece of evidence in the chapter, or does it add new evidence?

10 FACTS ABOUT ANCIENT EGYPT
abdocorelibrary.com/egyptian-mythology

Moving the Abu Simbel temple helped preserve it for future generations to visit.

FAST FACTS

Gods and Goddesses

- Bastet was a cat goddess. She was often pictured with the head of a cat or lioness.

- Osiris was the god of the dead.

- Horus, often depicted as a falcon, was the son of Osiris.

- Isis, the wife of Osiris, was a role model for Egyptian women.

- Maat was both a goddess and an important concept in ancient Egypt. The goddess was a symbol of truth and justice.

- Ra was the Egyptian sun god. He was also the king of all other Egyptian gods.

- Seth was a symbol of opposition and chaos. His role helped to explain why conflict and disagreement exist in the world. His popularity in Egyptian culture likely came from the people's appreciation for balance and harmony.

Creatures

- The sphinx had the body of a lion with the head of another being. Many sphinx statues have the heads of Egyptian rulers.

- Griffins have the body of a lion and the head of a bird. They are sometimes seen alongside sphinxes.

- A snake is often seen on the crowns of Egyptian rulers. A symbol of protection, this creature is called the uraeus.

Stories
- The story of the death of Osiris is one of the most important stories of Egyptian mythology. It explains how Osiris came to rule the underworld.

- The Eye of Ra is linked to several different goddesses—Hathor, Bastet, and Wadjet.

- The story of the shipwrecked sailor is one of the few Egyptian myths that feature human beings.

STOP AND
THINK

Say What?

Studying Egyptian mythology can mean learning a lot of new vocabulary. Find five words in this book that you had not seen before. Use a dictionary to find out what they mean. Then write the meanings in your own words, and use each word in a new sentence.

You Are There

This book talks about several well-known Egyptian myths. Imagine that you witnessed one of these stories yourself. Write a letter home telling your family and friends about your experience. Be sure to add plenty of details.

Surprise Me

Chapter Three talks about animals and other creatures of Egyptian mythology. What facts about these creatures surprised you the most? Write a few sentences about each fact. Why did you find them surprising?

Another View

This book discusses the role mythology played in Egyptian culture. As you know, every source is different. Ask an adult to help you find another source about this topic. Write a short essay comparing and contrasting the new source's point of view with that of this book's author. What is the point of view of each author? How are they the same? How are they different?

GLOSSARY

archaeologist
a scientist who studies human cultures of the past by examining objects left behind, such as pottery or buildings

deity
a god or goddess

hieroglyph
a symbol used in ancient Egyptian writing

inscribe
to write or carve words or symbols into something

marsh
an area of land that is typically wet and soft

mummify
to preserve a dead body through a drying process

polytheism
the worship of multiple gods and goddesses

righteous
without sin

venomous
able to inflict a poisonous bite

ONLINE
RESOURCES

To learn more about Egyptian gods, heroes, and mythology, visit our free resource websites below.

Visit **abdocorelibrary.com** for free Common Core resources for teachers and students, including vetted activities, multimedia, and booklinks, for deeper subject comprehension.

Visit **abdobooklinks.com** for free additional online weblinks for further learning. These links are routinely monitored and updated to provide the most current information available.

LEARN
MORE

Napoli, Donna Jo. *Treasury of Egyptian Mythology.* Washington, DC: National Geographic, 2013.

Zuchora-Walske, Christine. *Engineering the Pyramids of Giza.* Minneapolis, MN: Abdo, 2018.

INDEX

About the Author

Tammy Gagne has written dozens of books for both adults and children. Her recent titles include *Women in Engineering* and *Exploring the Southwest*. She lives in northern New England with her husband, son, and pets.